Mandeer, It's Magic!

John Pepper

Mandeer, It's Magic!

John Pepper

Illustrations by
Ralph Dobson

Appletree Press

*for Brian and Joan
- to remind them of some old
familiar sounds*

First published and printed by
The Appletree Press Ltd
7 James Street South
Belfast BT2 8DL
1986

British Library Cataloguing in Publication Data
Pepper, John
Mandeer, it's magic!
1. English Language—Dialects—Northern Ireland
Rn: Frederick Gamble
I. Title
427'.9416   PE2586
ISBN 0-86281-160-0

Contents

The Voice of the People

Once I heard it suggested — possibly with tongue in cheek — that there is an obvious reason why Northern Ireland should keep turning out such a string of world champions; for example in boxing, snooker, motor-cycle racing, athletics, indoor bowls, hot rod racing, flute playing and so on.

It's the way Ulster people talk, it was said. So often it causes such utter bewilderment that it becomes a matter of resorting to action if you're to be noticed. It is beyond doubt, however, that the Ulster way of putting things often causes problems.

'A prolonged whine,' a national television critic bluntly complained about the accent in his comment on a BBC play broadcast from Belfast. 'To the outsider it must be one of the ugliest and most unpenetrable,' it was stated. 'It often borders on the incomprehensible,' was another complaint. The people were described as dour, their speech 'like a foreign tongue.'

It may be that there is ground for such an indictment when a woman describes an encounter with her old friend, Lizzie McWhirter, by saying, 'When I saw her I said to myself, "Slizzie",' or the statement is heard, 'We were all set to move into our new house on Thursday but we put it aff for it was comin' down,' when the speaker merely meant that it was raining heavily. Similarly, the invitation 'Come round and have a slice of apple tart on your knee' can cause confusion if taken literally, just as will the suggestion 'Will you have a cup of tea in your hand?'

When I sought the opinions of a distinguished Englishman and an eminent Welshman, each with wide experience of the quirks of Ulster speech, their views were considerably at variance with those of the TV critics.

James Prior, Northern Ireland Secretary of State for a stretch of three years, confessed that at first he found it quite difficult to fully grasp what people said. 'Certainly the use of some words gives the outsider a misleading impression,' he said. 'I dare say, though, that the same criticism could be applied to a number of rural areas of Britain, for example the north-east coast and the shipyards. 'I do not think the Northern Irish are a dour lot. In fact I thought that on any subject other than politics they were good humoured and convivial. Perhaps I am a shade deaf but I thought they spoke softly at times.

'There is, however, a willingness to laugh at oneself which I found totally endearing during my time there and quite contrary to experience on the mainland.'

Merlyn Rees, within continuous earshot of the voice of Ulster for two and a half years in the same post, declared emphatically, 'It is not a whine.'

'Some vowels are elongated but why not?' he asked. 'Television critics tend to be metropolitan people from Hampstead (London) or Holywood (Co. Down). But then I am not a television critic nor a Southern Englishman. Try understanding a strong Yorkshire accent.

'I did not find the people dour or suspicious of outsiders, and so they should be. Outsiders think they have the answer to Ireland. Nobody in Ulster really believes that.

'In any event each country has its distinctive accent. On the North Coast the older people have a lilting, soft accent akin to that of the Western Isles.'

Another comment from someone who should know what he is talking about was from Professor James Milroy, of Sheffield University, formerly Senior Lecturer in English at Queen's University, who has published a textbook for the Northern Irish student of English phonetics.

'Belfast people should be proud of the way they talk,' he says. 'The Belfast accent may be a little exotic to some people but it is both lively and colourful, an accent to be proud of.'

In these pages, aided by a wide range of examples, it is sought to show that the Ulster idiom — what a critic might call the whine of the country — with its considerable Elizabethan, Scottish and Gaelic ingredients, offers rich rewards for all linguistic voyeurs.

Dacter, Dacter

'You're Mrs Savage? Mrs Martha Savage? And what's your trouble?' Dr Joseph Doherty searched through his files.

'I thought I'd have a wee word with you, dacter. Over my nerves? Is there something you could give me? It's my man.'

'So what has he been doing to you? Misbehaving? Beating you up?'

'No dacter. Nathin' like that. That's one thing about John. He'd nivver raise a hand to you.'

'So what is it then? Eating you out of house and home? Drinking?'

'He's drivin' me up the walls so he is. He has me that I don't know where to turn. The other night there I was goin' out and I said to him, "Bye now" and he wanted to know what I wanted him to buy now. Was there a sale on? Then he starts laughin' his head aff. That's the way he gets on all the time. Makin' silly oul jokes. He thinks he's a comedian who has only to be discovered and he'd be up there with Benny Hill and Frank Carson. He's a born ijit. He never staps.'

'But, Mrs Savage, surely it's only a bit of harmless fun?'

'Ach maybe it would be bearable if it was only in wee doses. But see him? He goes on and on, day and night, day in day out. He's drivin' me mad. He's drivin' the whole family mad. The gasman came the other day there to read the meter and he says to the poor man, "I suppose you're a leading light in the department?" '

10

'Did the man not make light of it?'

'A woman ast me if it wasn't heartenin' to have a man like him about the house. "A joke a minute," she says. "I wish my oul man would sparkle like that. All my man does is wine." I gave the woman a luck so I did. "Heartenin'," I said. "Its more like heart breakin'." Listen dacter. First thing in the mornin' he'll say, "Great day for the race," and just because I once ast him, "What race? Is it the Gran' National?" he thinks I'll keep on askin' and give him the chance to say, "No, woman, its the human race. Did you think I meant rice puddin'?" '

'Surely you're making a mountain out of a molehill?'

'Once I ast him to call me at eight and he says, "What do you want me to call you a Tate for?" He just can't get it out of his thick head that he's a rare turn. He makes me feel like I've commited bigamy or somethin' and married Little and Large. He gave me a packet of them waterproof plasters to give to the woman next door. I ast him why I should do that and he said, "Didn't you tell me that when the minister called and she had her curlers in she was all cut?" '

'That was thoughtful, I suppose, in a way.'

'Makes me sick to my stummick. He'll read out of the paper that they have a bus where you can have a test to see if your blood pressure is all right and he'll call it "A bus after your own heart" and laugh his head aff. At the hairdresser he was ast, "Do you want your hair done down the back?" and he said, "Why, haven't you enough room here where I'm sittin'?" The butcher had a notice "No dogs please" and he asts the man, "Would cats please you better?" The next day he walks into the shap with our dog on its lead and when the butcher said, "Can't you read?" he told him, "But this is a bitch." '

'You have an unusual husband, I'll say that.'

'On Saturday when he was going off to see about our holidays he tells me, "I'm going along to have a word with

'*Didn't you tell me that when the minister called and she had her curlers in she was all cut?*'

the travail agent." I just don't know what's got intil him, what started it all. He said last night that he was thinkin' of going to the BBC for an audition and because my daughter ast him, "Would a sixth do?" he sulked. He'll say to people, "I never smoke till I waken in the mornin' ." A friend was visitin' us last week and she said her brother had a wee farm. What does he say to her? He says, "A weave arm. What kind of an arm is a weave one?" The woman didn't know where to look. Last week there I went off to stay with my sister in the country for a couple of days and he leaves a note for the milkman, "Leave only one for the half of us aren't there." On and on he goes, dacter. Is there nathin' a body could do?'

'I have to say this. It's a problem I've never had to deal with before. Obviously you find it a strain, but how long have you been married now?'

'Twenty-five years, dacter.'

'You feel it's long enough, maybe? Is that it?'

'But he wasn't always like this. He used to be normal. Right enough, the day we were married and he was asked, "Do you take this woman?" up there at the altar he says "Yes minister." He said afterwards he was sorry, that he couldn't resist it, blamed it on the BBC. I was very annoyed. There must be some cure, dacter?'

'I'm afraid I can't say right off what it might be.'

'Will I bring him to see you?'

'Please no, Mrs Savage. I don't think that's the answer. I have a fair idea what his trouble is. He's a chronic comic. It's very unusual but not all that rare.'

'Before I left him reading the paper this morning he says, "I didn't realise Harry McCrudden the plumber is a Piscean. I wonder if that's why he likes chips?" I just didn't bother my head. The last time Mrs Crispin was in to see me I said to her, "I'll see yout" when she was leaving and he says, "If I had proper glasses maybe I could see yout as well.

Yout must be worth seeing." Then the next thing I hear is about him goin' into a pub and astin' for a Dry Martini and a towel. When they want to know why he wants a towel he says, "Man dear, it's to dry the Martini." '

'There's one suggestion I might make, Mrs Savage. Tit for tat. It might work. Comics always repeat themselves. I remember one of them telling me that his great problem was to remember the gags that got the laughs last week but got nothing but dead silence this week.'

'He nivver repeats himself. That's the trouble. The other night he nearly had the family arrested. He was driving me and the daughter home when we were stapped at an Army checkpoint. "Who are you?" the soldier asts us. "We're all Savages," says my husband.'

'All I can say is that you try giving him a dose of his own medicine and see what effect it has. Show him your nails and tell him you're thinking of entering a talon competition. Try that on him.'

'A talon competition, dacter? I don't understand.'

'Maybe that's not such a good idea. How about this one, then? Is he fond of fish?'

'We have it every week. He loves haddick.'

'Ask him if he'd do a bit of shopping for you next week. Ask him to go round to the fish shop and ask the man if he knows his place. Come back and let me know what happened.'

'What makes you think he doesn't know his place, dacter?'

'Just get him to try it anyhow, Mrs Savage.'

'All right, dacter. We'll see. I'll come back. If I still have my wits about me I'll come back.'

A Bit of a Change

Agnes Abernethy, staying in London with her sister-in-law, writes a letter home to her brother, Robert, in Belcoo:

Dear Robert,

As we mentioned the last time you drapped in on us, me and Harry is staying with Sam and his family here in Highgate in London for a wee bit of a break. Then we go to Eastbourne to stay with Eileen and her husband.

It's all a bit of a change from home. Everything's different. They don't even sell sodas. I went into a bread shop and asked for two sodas and they said they didn't keep mixers. Did you ever hear the like of it? I thought they weren't foreigners over here but sometimes I'm not so sure. They keep giving me funny looks every time I open my mouth. I'm nearly afraid to speak, so I am.

Sam had some of the neighbours in to meet us and I was talking about the terrible weather at home before we left. I said my back was all slates. 'Your back?' they asked and give Harry a quare look. He had to start in and tell them what I meant. They split their sides so they did. I felt terrible.

Then I said I thought it was a funny thing about Highgate. 'You nivver wash your front down,' I said. For a minnit nobody spoke. I knew they thought I'd said somethin' funny. I felt awful. Poor Harry had to start explainin' again. You feel like a right ijit.

I hardly spoke for the rest of the night and then Harry goes away an has them holdin' their sides again. We were talking about the way I'd seen a fella pinch a woman's handbag at a bus stop and what I called out to a bobby. All I done was to shout out, 'Hi, her hambeg's neucked.' You shudda heard them. I cudda seen Harry far enough. 'Hambeg neucked,' they shrieked and rolled about. 'What language is that?' they wanted to know. 'Mebbe it was Bantu,' they roared. I felt terrible ashamed.

A wee while after, somebody said it was gettin' late and one of the wimmen ast me the time. I told her I wasn't sure but I thought it was rightly on. 'You're a scream,' she said. 'Rightly on? What time is that when you're at home?' It took me all my time to stap myself from givin' her a slap across the gub.

Still I suppose it takes all sorts. We started talkin' about some of the people Sam knew in Belfast and there was this womman who had a lot of childer an' I was sayin' I nivver forgot what somebody said when she had her fourth son. 'That's one for every corner,' they said, an' when it hadda be explained that it meant she had a son for the four corners of her coffin when she was bein' buried they said they could hardly believe their ears. They thought it was hilarious. Then when I tried to remember her name and I couldn't an' said, 'Sure she was a wee woman with feet' they started shriekin' all over again.

When Sam told them that when she was bad somebody heard the health visitor sayin', 'Four sons or not it'll be a right sprachle to get her coffin down them narrow stairs,' you cudda heard the laughs of them a mile away. When they were goin' they said they nivver had a night like it, that their sides were sore.

Ye know me, I can't keep my big mouth shut. I was tellin'

Sam about Mrs Henry who used to live round the corner from us. One day a friend said to her that her son was fairly growin' up and it wouldn't be long before he'd be thinkin' of marryin'. 'I don't think he would,' she said. 'He has always been an innocent class of a young lad.' Sam said, 'It takes you back. It takes you back,' and give a big sigh.

But that's the trouble about bein' away from your own people, an' bein' with strangers. They have their wee ways and so have we. Me an' Harry went for a bit of a dander and we went that far I was dead bate when we got back. He knew I had a bad leg and when we were at our supper he ast me how it was for he was worried. 'Skillinmay,' I said and I was quaren relieved none of the Highgate people heard me or they would have went through the roof. It was outa me before I knew.

All the same I got my own back on one of them. She was talkin' about palatics and I heard her say, 'It's all the fault of the gumment.' I says, 'You mean government, don't you?' and she gave me a funny wee look. She nivver answered me.

Annest, though, it was the same in Eastbourne. The place was all right, but give me Donaghadee any day. I'd hardly time to warm the chair before they were on to me because I said, 'Harry likes dip.' Imagine it, they nivver heard of dip before! I cudden believe it. You'd think they weren't civilised. It was the same when I was talkin' about the way you have to clean the house if you have visitors an' I said I was often sorely tempted to make do with givin' the rooms a wee lick. I could see them raisin' their eyebrows.

Lizzie an' her man tuk us out for a meal and, just tryin' to be nice an' chatty, I said to the wee waitress, 'Sharry', for it had been rainin' on an' aff all day. 'Sweet or dry,' she says, and I was fairly thankful that Harry was there to come to my rescue.

I saw that the couple at the next table were starin' at us when I said to him, 'It's a good job I thu on a coat'. They

'I said I was often sorely tempted to make do with givin' the rooms
a wee lick.'

lucked again when Harry was talkin' to Lizzie about Joe Cahill and she ast him who Joe was for she didn't remember him. 'Surely you mind Joe?' Harry said. 'His farr drove a public convenience from Coleraine station for years.' I thought the pair at the next table were goin' to explode.

Annest, I near ast them if they wanted to move their table closer so they wudden miss anything. I just nivver ignored them. I passed the remark to Harry that it was a pity it was wet for I was a terrible dirty walker, that it was all them japs. It was great to have Lizzie and her husband to talk to and to be able to talk natural like and not have to transalate ivvery word you said.

We had Mickey Ronney, which is what Harry always calls that stringy Italian stuff. It was lovely. It's nice when it's well done. Just the job. I said it out loud so that themmuns at the next table cud hear and rack their brains over what I meant. But that's all for now.

Love,
Agnes

The Passing of Big Sam

When the Reverend Harry McMaster was faced with conducting the funeral of Sam Fortingale he knew he had problems.

The trouble was that Big Sam was a character. Every townland has one, some of them larger than others. Sam in many ways was out on his own. Everyone had a story about him. When people spoke of Sam it was always made to sound as if italics were needed. No one merely said 'Big Sam'. It was invariably 'Big Sam. Heh! He's the boy!'

If in Sam's eyes a woman was well put together he reckoned she was fair game, a challenge. He had a talent for turning a feminine head, and took full advantage of it. If he had many reluctant admirers among the ladies he had a fair number of enemies among the menfolk because of it. If a girl was spoken for it made no difference. One wrathful husband tore into Sam in the street. He finished up with a broken nose and a black eye, besides a badly punctured ego. Sam was unmarked — and unrepentant.

One of his adventures was to get himself locked in the local Bank of Ireland strongroom, where he spent the night.

'All that money at my finger tips,' he said afterwards, 'and all I could think of was that it was an awful pity that it wasn't a woman instead. There's no fun in taking a pile of banknotes in your arms.'

The bank manager didn't try to make an issue of the

incident but ever afterwards he made a personal check of the strong-room before he left the bank.

Sam managed to get two local girls in the family way, but there was no scandal. One got rid of the baby, as it was put. The other moved somewhere else with her family and was never heard of again. Sam took it all in his stride.

That he should eventually make his way to the altar took the wind out of everyone's sails. 'He's a boy,' they murmured again.

When the Reverend McMaster put the question at the wedding, 'Do you take this woman to be your lawful wedded wife, to love and cherish, to have and to hold, from this day henceforth?' Sam retorted, 'Sure that's what I'm here for.'

A little more than a year later his bride, Mary, died in childbirth. Sam was clearly upset. For weeks he kept to himself. It was thought that he had been tamed at last. Hardly a woman in the district didn't feel sorry for him. There was somehow more sympathy for Sam than mourning for Mary. Before long, however, he started drinking more heavily than ever. And he still showed he had an eye for a good-looking woman.

Eventually a husband complained to the Reverend McMaster. Something would have to be done about Sam, he claimed. He should be put away. It wasn't right. Sam was called to the manse.

'People are talking about you,' Sam was told. 'You just can't start behaving like a stud even if you feel like one. You're heading for serious trouble. For God's sake man, try and behave. In this day and age you can't go around acting as if you have the looks of John Wayne and the morals of Errol Flynn. Will you listen to me?'

'It isn't all my fault, Reverend,' Sam said. 'What's the harm in a wee bit of fun if the women get a wee bit of a kick out of it?'

'Sam! Don't be an ijit. You can't go about making a

nuisance of yourself and expect to get away with it just because you're handy with your fists when a man gets the rag out about you. You're becoming a damned nuisance, I'm warning you, Sam.'

'Sure, Reverend' Sam said, 'I know you're right. But it isn't always me. It's them. Sure they won't leave me alone.'

'Ach, come on now, Sam. This is your last warning. Look at the night you walked into a ladder and fell so awkwardly that you broke your leg, and the doctor asked you in the hospital what you had to drink and you said, "Five pints and three double vodkas." The man had to tell you he couldn't do a thing for you until the next morning. Catch yourself on.'

'I'll mend my ways, Reverend,' Sam said. 'You'll see.'

As Sam departed, the Reverend McMaster sighed and said to himself, 'Waste of time talking to him. The only thing that'll cure Sam is for him to be locked away somewhere.'

It was shortly after the talk that Sam was driving home in his seven-year-old Cortina following a heavy night. It was wet and foggy. The Cortina could not be called a fast car. It was fast enough to hit a telegraph pole with sufficient force to send Sam's head through the windscreen. He was a man who didn't believe in seat-belts.

But even in death Sam continued to be a problem.

The Reverend McMaster was a cleric with a strong belief in being realistic in what he said about the deceased at the funeral. He had strong feelings at the way some clerics would steer clear of an honest assessment of a late member of the congregation.

Why should it always be flattering, he often asked himself. The departed had always to be beyond reproach. How to get round saying Sam was nothing more than a playboy? Likeable, but still a playboy? A man who made some people happy but made many unhappy. In the

'*Let us pray.*'

congregation would be husbands who hated Sam's guts, all of them upright men.

Women outnumbered men at the funeral service. The Reverend McMaster faced them with some uneasiness.

'Big Sam, as it says on so many of the wreath cards today, has gone,' he told the mourners. 'He will now be facing his Maker. He deserves our sympathy. He could have done more with his life, as it can be said of all of us when we are called above.'

The Reverend McMaster was on the verge of adding, 'He will be missed,' but did not utter the words, even if he recognised they were fully justified. They were words that were always justified. How could he say them about Sam as if speaking of a virtue? Instead he murmured, 'Let us pray.'

The
Nine-to-One On

Ask a Belfast shipyardman to voice an opinion and he won't hesitate about doing so. What he has to say may not reach startling metaphysical heights but the language he uses will have lively, original qualities of its own.

When the Greek ship IXION was being built by Harland and Wolff the name was never heard mentioned. This was not because of any difficulty in pronouncing it. The labour force follows the horses to a man and never referred to the vessel other than as 'The nine-to-one on.'

The search for a different way of putting things is part and parcel of their philosophy. A player in one of the lunch-break card games always indicated that he would wait for the others before declaring what he would do with his cards by saying, 'I'll let the hare sit.' This explains why he always answered to Myxamatosis, although his name was David.

Clashes with authority produce the inevitable sparks. An overseer was greeted by his former shopfloor workmates on the morning after his promotion, 'And how's our Sammy this morning?' He stopped and sternly addressed them, 'Look I've been promoted. I'm in a position of authority now. I expect to be treated with some respect. I'm Sammy no more.' Ever after he was known as 'Sammy No More'.

An unduly pompous foreman, angry at what he considered lack of respect from a welder he was rebuking, demanded, 'Look, do you know who I am?' The welder turned to his mates and grinned, 'Hi lads. Here's a fella doesn't know who he is.'

This scorn for authority was marked by the graffiti scrawled on a ship's side after the announcement that the then chairman of the Yard was to receive a knighthood. 'Work for the Knight is coming' it read. It was during a period when orders were at their lowest and wage rates had been pared to the bone. The story, probably apocryphal, is told that when receiving the accolade at the Palace the Queen said to him, 'Arise Sir ————' three times without result. An aide then whispered, 'Better just tell him to get up. Where he comes from they don't know what a rise means.'

When an overseer was the recipient of the BEM his persistence in checking on work in progress was indicated by his name chalked prominently on a wall followed by the words 'Back Every Minute'.

An executive spotted a worker dodging through the Yard gates long before finishing time. When spoken to the man said, 'Chaze, Mister, I'm only a wee bit early. Why can't you mind your own business?'

'Do you know who I am?' the executive demanded.

'No,' said the workman. 'Do you know who *I* am?'

'I don't,' said the executive, bringing out his notebook.

'Thank God for that,' said the workman and took to his heels.

A painter who was seen arriving one morning in a gleaming new Cortina inspired the comment, 'God, but Hughie's rightly on his feet so he is.'

In fact speech patterns have changed little down the years since Belfast's earlier troubles. In the twenties a visitor to the city was said to have narrowly escaped being hit by a stray bullet when a shipyard tram came under fire because he failed to understand the conductor's warning cry, 'Allayizjuke'.

'Allayizjuke.'

A philosophical approach to the risks that go with ship-building was reflected by the painter who fell from some scaffolding and told colleagues who rushed to his aid, 'Ach I'm all right. Sure I was comin' down anyway. I needed more paint.'

Another accident victim lamented as the ambulance was awaited, 'Looks like my football days are over.' Instantly he was told, 'Don't be silly, man. Sure you can still blow a whistle.'

Everyone who works under the towering Queen's Island cranes is fair game. A newly appointed management trainee, small in stature, luckily did not hear the remark made about him as he passed a group of workers, 'Wudden two of that wee character luck well on a mantelpiece?'

The years have not brought the end of the packed lunch, but what it consists of has changed with the times. One member of a welding squad grumbled to his colleagues as they opened their plastic boxes, 'God but I'm sick of cheese. It's always cheese.'

'Why don't you tell the missus to make something else?' he was told. 'That's what I would do.'

'What's the use,' came the reply. 'She won't even touch it. I always have to make it myself.'

The Gunking
of Thelma

The two girls were some distance down the bus queue. It was rush hour.

'There was this fella with dark hair,' Thelma said. 'Talked awful plite. Know what I'm goin' till tell you, Tania? He strikes up to me in the queue here last night. I was standin' tryin' to make up my mind whether I'd get my hair done on Friday when all of a sudden he turns round to me and says, "Goin' way anybody?" '

'He didn't, Thelma?'

'Anest. Near tuk the feet from under me. I said to him, "Goin' where?" You shud have seen the way he tossed his head to get his black hair outa his eyes. "Just goin' way anybody?" he said. "Like anor fella." '

'He had a nerve all right, Thelma.'

'I said to him, straight out like, "What business is it of yours?" His shoes were nice and clean and shiny. He had a wee bit of a lipse. "I was ony askin'," he said. "Smoke?" He affers me a Galliker's green.'

'He didn't, Thelma?'

'I told him "I don't mind," an' he brings out a tidy wee silver lighter. I just cudden place him. Looked like somebody that worked in Shorts.'

'All the same, Thelma. You have to watch out. Just because he offers you a Galliker's green doesn't mean he isn't one of them bra grabbers in his heart. Lats of them about.' '

'Anyway we lit up and he said, "I haven't seen you on a Braniel bus. Live there?" "Born there," I told him. He looked harmless. Nails nice and clean. Nice teeth. "Workin?" I asked him. "Don't make me laugh," he says. "I'm thinkin' about it. You never said if you were goin' way anybody." "What's it till you?" I asks. He had nice blue eyes, Tania. All the time there was this oul fella with a dirty tash watching us, listening till every word. I could have seen him far enough.'

'Some people just can't mind their own business, Thelma. Some people would make you sick so they would.'

' "If you aren't workin' where are you coming from?" I asked him. "Your social security?" '

' "Me and my mate were playin' snooker," he says. He kept shaking the hair out of his eyes every other minute. He was dishy, Tania. Anest. He told me he knew Hurricane Higgins. He says, "Workin' yourself?" I told him I was in Galliker's. "Gawd," he says, "and here's me handin' my fegs round like an ijit and you get them for nothing. I'm the right Charley. Goin' way anybody out of Galliker's?" "Sure they're nearly all girls there," I tells him. "Were you born yesterday?" I asks.'

'You didn't let him get away with anything, did you?'

'No fear, Tania. "Know a fellow called Larry that works there," he says. "A boyo. Smooth. Real smooth." I says, "There's a lotta them about. Think they have only to raise an eyebrow and people worship the ground they walk on." He laughed out loud. "You're a one," he says. "I fancy I'd have to do more than work the eyebrows to get you falling over." I says to him, "Sonny, you can say that again." Then he asks, "What's your name? Millicent? Angela? Henrietta? No, I don't think you're a Henrietta. Maybe Eileen?" So I tells him, "If you're all that anxious to know, it's Thelma. You have the look of a Sammy yourself. Or an Alec. But you're the dead spit of an Ernie." Then I said, "It isn't Liam?" '

'*I felt fairly gunked, so I did.*'

'And what was it? It wasn't Liam, was it?'

'It wasn't Liam. He said it was Brian. Anest, Tania, I stood there prayin' that the bus would be late and mebbe he'd want to date me. I had to see Jimmy that night and, know what I'm going to tell you? I'd have stood Jimmy up so I would. I'm going aff Jimmy.'

'You're not going aff Jimmy, Thelma. I don't believe you.'

'He never even sent me a Valentine card. I was fairly hurt.'

'But the boyo with the dark hair, Thelma. You said it kep blindin' him? From where I'm standin' he wasn't the ony one being blinded.'

'Him?' Thelma shrugged. 'You won't believe this but he brings out one of them toothpicks and starts pickin' his teeth in front of me. A toothpick! I minded my haroscope said I should look out for a setback. I felt fairly gunked, so I did. Shows you how wrong you can be.'

'Right enough, Thelma. You can never be sure from one minute till the next.'

'Anyway the bus came up and I says to him, "I'm fer aff" and just left him pickin' away at his oul teeth. I got a seat away at the back and just nivver ignored him. Sure he was nathin' but a put on.'

'You were just right, Thelma. I wonder whereabouts he lives in Braniel?'

Henry Something

It was a busy time on the Newtownards Road. The two housewives were making their way along the crowded Ballymacarret pavement, discussing the price of eggs, when one of them exclaimed, "See him, Bella? She pointed across the road. 'Him in the cap. He has a wee stoop.'

'Him in the cap? Looks a bit like Jerry Wogan.'

'Terry, Bella. Terry. I'd say he looks more like our milkman. But I've remembered. His name's Henry. An he's nat our milkman.'

'Henry what?'

'Henry something.'

'It wudden be Johnston? There's an awful lot of people called Johnston. They're everywhere. There's a Johnston lives next door till me. A traffic warden.'

'What on earth makes you think it's Johnston, Bella? It's Henry something. I'm sure of it.'

'Our coalman's called Johnston. McCracken Johnston. I always thought it was funny.'

'Away to hell, Bella.'

'I'm not making it up. It's the truth.'

'But this man, Henry something. I believe he's goin' intil that hairdresser's.'

'It's somewhere I'll have to be going. My hair's a sight.'

'I wish I could think of that man's name. It's bothering me. I won't have a minute's peace until it comes to me.'

'It wouldn't be Dewhurst? I think Dewhurst's a terrible nice name. This book I'm reading, it's about India and there's this man Dewhurst. He's a British officer and they have it in for him.'

'Don't be ridiculous, Bella.'

'This Henry. What does he do?'

'I know what he does all right. He has a terrible sad time of it. He's in an undertaker's. He walks alongside the hearse.'

'I often feel sorry for them people. Making a living out of looking as if it's the end of the world. Never able to have a wee bit of a laugh at his work. Maybe that's why he's going into the hairdresser's. In a job like that you have always to look respectable. It wouldn't do if he looked in need of a haircut.'

'I wish I could think of that name.'

'How do you know him anyway?'

'He's a friend of Jimmy's. They're in the same darts club. Jimmy brought him home one night. He was very interesting. He talked about his work. He said it took him a long time to get used to it. Once he won £150 on the pools and he had three funerals to do the same day. He said it was agony, having to wear a long face.'

'Still. It's the man's job. It's what he's paid for.'

'He told us about another bad day. It was an old woman's funeral. She was ninety-seven and he couldn't keep his eyes off the chief mourner who was wearing a black shoe and a brown one. As if that wasn't bad enough he had on different socks. You can imagine, Bella. Just think of trying to keep from splitting your sides at somebody like that.'

'It isn't the kind of job my man could hold down. He'd be laughin' his head off the whole way to the cemetery.'

'He was saying the whole trouble is that your entire life's affected by having to look down in the mouth day after day. When you're not at work you're dead scared to laugh if

'Just think of trying to keep from splitting your sides at somebody
like that.'

somebody says something funny to you. He told us if there's a comedian on television he switches to another channel. If only I could remember the man's name.'

'Forget it, Bella. Nivver bother yourself about it. It wouldn't be McGoldrick?'

'No, it isn't McGoldrick. The only McGoldrick I know is Alec. Nivver in the house. Always out playing indoor bowls.

'And does a lot of other things forby. I know the man well. Sold a car to a man my man works with. It was nothing but a bunla scrap. He was done in that car so he was.'

'You feel awful stupid when you can't think of somebody's name.'

'It'll come to you all right. It'll come to you when you're not thinking. But I'll have to go on, Sophie. I've got to go over to Smith's for sausages for the tea.'

'But that's it, Bella. Smith! Henry Smith! God, I'm glad it came to me. Henry Smith! Now I'll sleep tonight.'

Fancy a Jube-jube?

He was not a man who flew to London so regularly that he was able to start chatting to the passenger next to him without giving it some thought. This time Fred Gilfedder had an aisle seat on the shuttle beside a woman in that indeterminate group — under forty or just over it, and able to conceal it. Whatever the scent she was using it was pleasant. Not too obtrusive, he decided approvingly.

According to the pilot, the shuttle was flying at a height of some 55,000 ft at 600 miles an hour. Fred leaned back with a contented sigh, looking forward to being able to tell Ruth about the important people he'd met in London, and the interesting two days he'd had.

There was the chap who was a member of the Hurlingham Club and apparently often ran into Denis Thatcher at his golf club. The fellow who had taken him along to a House of Commons debate had been really decent. So had the company's secretary who had taken him along to dinner in a place called Keatings. It had been a real experience. One of the better trips to head office.

When it was a woman he was always dubious about breaking the ice. The experience nearly a year ago on a flight had been a warning. Impulsively he had said to the smartly dressed passenger on his right, who was reading the *Daily Mail*, 'A bit on the bumpy side today, isn't it?'

She did not answer but gave him an angry glare that

made him feel she was about to call the air hostess and complain of indecent assault. He broke into a cold sweat. Thinking about it could still make him shiver.

That occasion apart, he felt that not to be able to chat effortlessly to a stranger was a reflection on his ability to extract the maximum interest from a journey. He always remembered with warmth the man who was managing director of a clothing concern which sold 10,000 suits a year to Marks and Spencer. It was fascinating to listen to him.

And the MP who couldn't stand Esther Rantzen because of her teeth. It was a dislike they shared. It made such a difference when you encountered one of your own class, who enjoyed 'Mastermind' as much as you did yourself, and hated 'Dallas' and Kenny Everett.

The 'No Smoking' sign went out and as he undid his seat belt he was again aware of the woman's perfume. It had quite a fragrance. Delicate. He saw her search in her handbag and thought of offering her a cigarette, but she had produced a packet before he could reach for his own and the opportunity was gone.

From what he could see she looked highly respectable. Was probably in business. Maybe even a company manager; possibly a widow. Women nowadays were hard to assess. She had an air of efficiency about her. Her hands weren't rough.

He heard the drinks trolley approaching. If she had a gin and tonic it would be a useful clue. If she had a mineral it would also be a giveaway. He could say casually, 'We're having a nice smooth flight, aren't we?' The weather conditions always provided a safe subject. 'This is only my second flight on a Trident' could start the ball rolling. Or 'The service now is really good. It's the competition. It makes a difference.'

It had to be something that signalled he sought nothing more than a harmless chat. There was no other motive. He was a happily married man. Not interested in the chance of an extra-marital adventure like some of his friends at the golf club.

He turned slightly and stole a better look at her. She was certainly on the far side of forty, but well preserved. She had a nice figure, a woman who could look after herself. The sort of woman Ruth would sum up as a person to treat with respect. Looked as if she was married to a Rotarian, a man in a good way of business.

Interesting, he decided. The type Ruth would want to hear him talk about. She always approved if they were nice people, the sort you liked to mention to your friends.

All at once the decision was taken out of his hands. She started searching in her handbag. It was crammed with lipstick, a small diary, keys, a cigarette lighter, two blue handkerchiefs, two match booklets, another bunch of keys, some letters, a silver pencil, and other odds and ends. It was even worse than Ruth's.

He was suddenly aware that the woman had turned towards him and he found himself looking into her dark brown eyes.

'Fancy a jube-jube fer yer ears?' she asked 'You aren't one of them, are you? I don't think so or I wudden ask. Isn't this a bluddy stingy air line? You'd think they could afford a jube-jube on the house. A jube-jube can be the quare mark when yer flyin'.'

'Good God,' Fred Kilfedder thought frantically. He swallowed and stammered, 'Thanks all the same.' He reached desperately for the 'Instructions to Passengers' pamphlets. He could hear the rustle of paper as the woman extracted a jube-jube from the packet. It was something he wouldn't mention to Ruth, he decided, and read that a life jacket was under his seat. He had a feeling that the scent in his nostrils had somehow become niffy.

Meeting with a Chancer

The bar was quiet for it was early in the evening. The frowning, slim man in the tweed cap, a half-empty glass in front of him, was staring at the array of bottles on the other side of the counter as if the display offended him.

Jimmy, low set, bare-headed, came in and called to the barman, 'Dross a pint.' He moved up beside the lone drinker. 'Alec,' he said, his voice flat. He made it sound as if Alec was there on false pretences.

'Jimmy.' Alec drew the back of his hand across his mouth. He did not look up. There was no enthusiasm in his tone. 'Fancied I'd run intil ye.'

'Did ye now? And why was that?' The new arrival was overweight and balding.

'Luck, man. Quit yer coddin'. Ye said things about me, so ye did. Called me a chancer.' The voice was resentful and challenging. 'Didden ye say I was a chancer?'

'All I said was that you did all right when the goin' was dicey. Man dear, we're all in the same boat when Hardy comes to Hardy.'

'Jesus but you hev a nerve. A right bluddy nerve. Know somethin', I've a bluddy good mine to break that jaw of yours. Callin' me a chancer!' Alec tugged at the peak of his cap. 'For two bluddy ticks I'd thump the linin' outa ye.'

'Howl on, man. Just howl on. Say anor flippin' word and I'll rearrange that face of yours.'

'Man but ye'd need a latta help, so ye wud. A helluva lat.' Alec raised his glass, studied it for a moment, then drank. Carefully he put it down. 'This isn't a buck ijit yer talkin' to.'

'Man dear, yer nathan but a wee lightweight. Ye'd be cryin' for mercy once I gat started on ye. Shriekin' for it. Callin' out for Scottie to beam you up.'

'Where did ye get that idea?'

'Don't you worry yer thick head where I gat it.' Jimmy took a long drink. 'Ye'd be wee buns. Ye'd have no chance.' he rubbed his bald head.

'Get a grip on yerself. If I raise a hand till ye yer finished. Done. Ye'd be lyin' there spread out like a lettuce.'

'You an' who else? Tell me that. God but ye were always the quare geg when it comes till talk. Talk's cheap.'

'Look. Have a titter of wit. I know ye. Takes me all my time to set ye back on yer behin' here and ni so it does. Say anor word and ye'll think McGuigan had shoved yer jaw down yer throat. Ye'll be goin roun' luckin' for a face transplant. That head of yours'll be like a bap.'

'Watch yerself, boy. Just watch yerself.' Noisily Jimmy tapped the counter with his glass, a man holding himself back.

'In the name of Gawd what do you want me to watch myself for? I'm nat goin' till start shavin'. I shaved this mornin'.'

'Givvus anor pint,' Alec called to the barman, his teeth clenched. He kept looking straight ahead. 'I doan know what's keepin' me from pinnin' this bluddy man's ears back. Sure he's nathan more than a parcel of bad meat.' He turned to his adversary. 'Just let me get started and by the time I've finished way ye ye'll be hirplin' up till your bed bent double for a week.'

'Huh,' Jimmy sneered. 'Boy but ye're goin' well the night. See that mug of yours. The kinda treatment I'll give it'll cripple ye for the rest of yer days. Mine ye, I'm not boastin'.'

'Bitta trouble, Hughie?'

'Ach.' The glass was raised to Alec's lips. 'Doan make me laugh. After I've dealt with ye ye'll be lyin there like a deceased pigeon.'

'Sure yer nathan but a slabber. A born slabber.' Jimmy spoke like a man delivering a carefully worked out judgment.

The barman put Alec's change on the counter. 'When are you pair goin' till run outa theats? We doan like theatenin' language in this bar. This is a respectable place. Just watch it.'

Jimmy looked up. 'I didden come here till be insulted. I thought you didden allow gits in this bar.'

'Watch it, boy,' the barman said. 'Take it easy.'

'Yer wastin' yer time,' Alec said. 'He's makin' me sick till my stummick. It's the Gawd's truth. The man's all mouth.'

'I came in here for a quiet pint. That was all. All I get is dog's abuse.' Jimmy made a gesture of despair.

'You called me a chancer.' Alec was like a dog with a bone he refused to let go.

'For Gawd's sake, give over,' Jimmy protested. 'I didden say ye were a pain in the arse. I didden say that, did I?'

'You didden. All the same.'

A man in a corduroy jacket came in. He called to the barman, 'Battle by the neck.' He kept his distance from the antagonists.

'Sure,' the barman said.

The new arrival said to him in low tones, 'Bitta touble, Hughie?'

'A bit,' the barman conceded.

'They don't sound as if they think much of each other.'

The barman served the order. 'Ach they've been theatenin' to bate the livin' daylights outa each other for as long as I can remember. It's a kinda habby they tuk up. He looked towards the two men.

Alec was saying, 'Yer nathan but a born blirt.'

'Make no mistake abut it,' Jimmy replied. 'Once I get

43

goin' on them two ears I'll put them where your mouth is. That face will luck like a welder's glove. It'll be an improvement on that gub of yours, so it will.'

The barman shrugged. 'Lissen to them', he told the corduroy jacket. 'Married to two sisters, them two. They don't get on. Let it be a lesson to you.'

Mountainy Low-down

It is a fair distance from Carrickfergus to Carolina, or from Tempo to Tennessee. To Sean, from Newtownards, it didn't seem all that far once he got there.

He and Richard had set out in a hired car to cover as many American states as they could in six weeks. They found America fascinating and the roads long, but often encountered the usual look of bewilderment when they spoke. Once when they asked the way and were given detailed instructions Sean sought to voice his thanks to their guide for going to so much trouble.

'Squaren ice of you to go to all this borr,' he said.

'Ice?' the man echoed. 'Ice?'

'We're beholden to you,' Richard explained.

After that they were careful about what they said until they went into a cafe in Tennessee. It was crowded and they had to share a table with two housewives. The women's conversation soon had Sean gasping.

'I can't abide them kinda folk,' he heard one of the women say.

'Me neither,' replied the other. 'I don't know for why, mind you. I jes can't.'

'Makes my teeth scringe,' said the first woman as Sean began to think he was back home again. 'The sort that would argify the whole night.'

'When I see them I nivver let on. It's the only way.'

'Squaren ice of you to go to all this borr.'

'Nobody would fault you for that,' came the agreement. 'But you look a bit peaked this morning.'

'I have a bad stomach, that's for why. Between that and a bad tooth.'

'I never had no trouble with my teeth. They just rotted out naturally. Haven't you seen the doctor?'

'No I have not,' the second woman said. 'I pay no mind to that man. I went to see him when my face was all swole up. I'd been ailing for weeks but I got nowhere. He's all right for the rheumatiz but I wouldn't be beholden to him for anything else. The man next door saw him and he was very put out.'

'He's gettin' dotey. That year the river friz over he said he was plumb wore out he had that much to do. He's no use. That man wudden know a crick in the neck from a broken leg.'

The second woman pushed back her plate. 'Maybe it's time we riz. I hev all the reddin' up to do.'

Sean could hold back no longer. 'Tell me, are youse from Norn Iron?'

'Norn Iron?' The woman who answered made it sound like a village in Siberia. 'We've lived in these parts all our lives.'

As the couple left the waitress arrived with a menu. Inside was what was described as a glossary of 'Mountainy Talk'. This, it was explained, consisted of words 'used by people living in the mountain area bordering North Carolina and Tennessee'.

Sean read that 'Doins' means 'A function' as in 'Are you goin' to the church doins tonight?' He discovered that, as in Co. Down, 'You'ns' means 'you' or 'you all'.

Richard found that 'A fur piece down the road' has the same meaning that it has in Conlig, as does 'It smarts where I got hit'.

'Fairly makes you feel at home,' Sean said.

'Dussent it?' Richard agreed. 'It's a small world.'

Just then a man at the next table exclaimed to his companion, 'It was done unbeknownst to me.'

Sean looked across at him. 'Any minnit now we'll see a wee lad comin' in sellin' *Baird's Tele.*'

The Key of Hell

Anyone who stopped a passer-by in a Belfast street and said, 'I'm looking for the key of hell; where do I go?' would risk a dusty answer if the person consulted did not happen to be a native. A resident of the city would know at once that Cave Hill was being sought. Try saying it with the 'cave' drawn out and the confusion is apparent.

Similar perplexity can be caused to the outsider on hearing someone say, 'My man just loves gettin' aff thawday.' This is not a reference to a religious holiday. 'Thawday' is another word for the odd, or occasional, day off work. It is equally pleasant to get off 'thawed week' or even 'thawed Friday'.

In the same convoluted style there was the public library assistant who observed that each book a woman returned had the word 'Freddit' written unobtrusively on the fly leaf.

'What does it mean?' the woman was asked.

'Augh it's only to remind me that I've had the book out before, that I've read it.'

A guest of whom it will be said, 'He stood for a whole half hour with the door in his hand' is not a Mr Universe who likes showing off. The statement is nothing more than a reference to those people who tend to prolong their departure, the kind who insist on standing talking interminably at the open door, gripping the handle, before taking a reluctant departure. Unfortunately there is no known cure for turning the business of saying goodbye into a long drawn out performance.

Also apt to confound those unaccustomed to Ulster idiomatic variations is 'I was terrible sorry I had to come home so soon for my legs were just beginning to turn.' All the speaker was seeking to convey was that she had been on a holiday in Spain and was regretting that her stay in the sun had not been long enough to give her legs a deep all-over tan. It could have been that the lady was not for turning. She just wasn't given the time.

To overhear a bus passenger tell her companion, 'They've never married so they haven't,' and the query, 'Won't he turn?' won't make it easy not to keep listening.

It will be no help when the reply comes, 'Turn? He wouldn't even turn green if he was as sick as a dog.' What is meant is that the man is firm in his reluctance to change his religious beliefs.

No age group is immune from this vocal perversity. The small boy who told his mother tearfully, 'She lay intil me with a pointer' was explaining that the teacher had used a school pointer instead of the usual cane for corrective treatment. What it did to his English is clear.

'Are you getting?' is not the kind of inquiry apt to be put to a shopper in the average English store. When it was put to a visiting businessman in a Belfast shop his wife gave him a look of alarm. She wondered anxiously if the assistant was displaying an unduly inquisitive interest in the more intimate side of his married life. To her relief he told the girl, 'Thanks, we're just browsing,' and all was well.

Ask in a Belfast Post Office for 'a book of second rate stamps' and the assistant won't turn a hair. Second class and second rate are synonymous in the city, which seems a sensible assumption.

Yet there is every reason to assume that what happened in a Belfast hospital could have occurred just as easily in

'I'm the man with the gravel.'

one in England. A sister on her rounds was approached by an individual who said, 'I'm the man with the gravel. Where do I go?'

She showed instant concern, told him to follow her, got in touch with a consultant, and for some moments caused a state of panic because no one could establish if 'gravel' was a serious complaint or something trivial. The crisis passed when it was found that the man was delivering a load of gravel for some road repairs at the hospital.

Misunderstandings are created so easily that they often seem to reflect slow thinking. In fact it is often a case of taking people literally. The invitation, 'Just put your fut in the bus and you'll be welcome any time' should be understood right away. Yet it can make people start asking themselves, 'Just how can I do that?'

Sawfly, Sawfly

Record of a conversation in a Belfast street between a visitor and a native of Northern Ireland following the controlled explosion of a suspect bomb:

'Diaballical.'

'Excuse me?'

'Shockin' sotis. More tex on pleece. Make ye sick.'

'I beg your pardon. I don't quite understand.'

'These tex. Y'know? Caracters hevvinago.'

'Hevvinago? I'm lost.'

'Beltin' intil the pleece. Cloddin'.'

'I'm still getting nowhere, I'm afraid. Could you perhaps start all over again?'

'Mandeer wud ye yewsyer loaf?'

'Ah, I get the message. Cockney rhyming slang. Loaf of bread, head.'

'Chase man! Cackney, y'say. I'm nat talkin' Cackney. Nofeer. Sher lugs, mister. Need singed.'

'Singed? I've lost you again.'

'Lost? Doan ye know where yare? Luck. I'll spellit out. Tex. It's what tarists do.'

'Tarists? Tarists? Oh, I see, You mean terrorists?'

'Rite, then. Mennavilence. When there's texon pleece it's themmuns. Alwaysis. Luckin' a knighted Iron.'

'Knighted Iron? You have a wonderful way of putting things. I'll say that.'

'Here's a fella clactin' fer narch.'

'Nathanup way it. Natifye lussen.'

'I'm listening most intently I can assure you. I'm most anxious to understand what you're trying to say. Believe me.'

'Tellus this. Waraye frum?'

'What do you mean?'

'Watta ast. Waraye frum?'

'I'm from Lancashire, actually.'

'Frens here?'

'We're here on business, as a matter of fact.'

'Gointill any matches?'

'If you mean football matches, no.'

'Yew back the Blues?'

'As a matter of fact I'm a supporter of Queen's Park Rangers. Purely for sentimental reasons.'

'Loada rubbitch. Nivver heerav the Week Lens?'

'Week Lens? Never, I have to confess. Are they good?'

'Mandeer they're magick. Skrate till luck at them on the feel. Jus skrate.'

'You think Queen's Park aren't in the same class?'

'Week Lens wud suck them up and blow them out again like bubbles. They're sintillatin'.'

'I'll take your word for it.'

'See my bror? Used to trane the Week Lens. The bror's no dozer. They can bate the Blues intil the groun'.'

'Is that a fact?'

'Beck the Week Lens an yer homandry.'

'Sorry . . . . You're away again.'

'Homandry. On th' ball. But howl on. Here's a fella clactin' fer narch.'

'A narch?'

'Nivver heerava narch?'

'To be frank, no. Never.'

'Nivver borr yer head then.'

'In any event you're an admirer of the Week Lens?'

55

'Pack them alla way. Manado.'

'I see. Anyway, thanks a lot for being so helpful. You've gone to a great deal of bother. You've helped to make things a great deal — well, clearer, I think. It was most interesting.'

'Snathan'.'

'You have explained everything so graphically. Thanks awfully.'

'Sawfly? You talkin' about Ruby Murray's hit? Sawfly, Sawfly?'

'Not really, I have to say. Thanks anyway. I think we'll just leave it there. Goodbye.'

The
Happy Medium

After Eileen Colhoun lost her man she was looked on as a bit of an oddity. She was all heart, but widowhood had changed her. No getting away from it, everybody agreed. She wasn't the same woman. Another thing; she didn't even wear black.

When she started telling people, 'I've heard from Frank,' it was taken as confirmation of the judgment. 'A pity about Eileen,' they said to each other, nodding. 'Imagine saying she's heard from him. Did you ever hear the like?'

Everything changed, however, the night of the meeting. For several days beforehand there were posters announcing that 'Carswell Cinnamond, world renowned medium' would be speaking at a public gathering to which all interested were invited. 'Can there be communication with the dead?' the posters challenged. 'Hear what Carswell Cinnamond has to say. It will be a revelation.'

The response was modest. The small hall was only half-filled, but the audience included Eileen. Many attended as much to see if she would be there and what would happen as to hear the man himself.

He had a hint of a Scottish accent which his mainly Presbyterian audience found appealing. Eileen's hand was one of the first to be raised when he invited anyone who had 'a friend who had passed on' if they would like to hear from them.

At first he explained that the spirit world was a crowded

place, not easily penetrated. Conditions had to be right, but he would be doing his best. He said he could do no better than that. It was at this stage that there was the collection 'to cover expenses'.

He first devoted his attention to Stewart Kernahan. Stewart's wife Esther had died from a coronary, leaving him with two children. Stewart thought it would be nice to have a message from her. Was she all right?

After some moments of furtive silence Carswell said, 'Conditions are fairly reasonable. They could be better but I can say that Esther wants to tell you how sorry she is that the call came. She says she hopes you are managing and not letting the children get out of hand. She says she wishes she could write to you about them.'

'Could you tell her that wee Christopher broke Mrs Kennedy's window?' Stewart asked.

'I'll try,' said the medium. 'But I'm afraid there is interference. I'm sorry.'

There was no great success in reaching Mrs McLusty's brother-in-law, but Mrs Agnes Mawhinney was told there was an improvement in spirit conditions and that her husband Peter was settling down. It was Eileen's turn and Carswell said there was a definite message from Frank.

'You're not to give in,' she was told. 'He wants you to know that he had a wonderful funeral and that the flowers were wonderful too. He says it was a nice service, that it couldn't have been better if he'd arranged it all himself.'

Eileen was delighted. After that her status took a turn for the better. She ceased to be considered an oddity. Before long it was being made known that she'd had a private talk with Carswell and that he had been most impressed by what she told him about hearing from Frank. Very impressed.

Next came the announcement that she had decided to set up as a medium herself. 'There isn't one for miles,' she said.

'There's only them ones that come for the one night and then they're away. That's no use.'

Came the night when she had her first séance. Eight people attended, two of them widowers, four of them widows. The others came 'out of curiosity'. It began with a cup of tea and 'a wee corn beef sandwich' for everyone, then 'a bit of a collection to pay for her trouble'. There had been more messages from Frank, she said, but she was sure people would want to hear from their own loved ones. What Frank had to say could wait.

First there was Mrs Tomelty, whose husband was dead eight years. 'Would you ask John if he minds if I sold his teeth?' she suggested nervously. After some moments Eileen said she was certain she had reached him. The connection was faint but strong enough for him to convey that he had no objections. 'You go ahead, Daisy,' he said, according to Eileen.

Mrs Crone, whose sister had been killed in a car crash, wanted to know if Olive had got rid of her bad leg. Back came the assurance that it no longer bothered her, it was as right as rain now.

Mrs Elder, widowed for six months, inquired, 'Could Jimmy tell me where he hid the half-bottle of port wine that was bought for Aggie McLoughlin's birthday party?' She had looked high and low for it.

At this stage Eileen indicated that she was afraid she was getting tired, that 'gettin' through takes a lot out of a body' and that anyhow she would be having another gathering. Everyone said they would be back. 'It was a grand night,' they said. 'Comfortin'.' It was on the tip of Eileen's tongue to say, 'I'm glad you all enjoyed yourselves' when she decided this wouldn't be the right way to put it.

That night she went off to bed wondering how she might handle the problem of the hidden half-bottle of port wine.

'Now if I could ask Frank,' she thought. 'It would be no

bother for him to find out. No bother at all.'

'Still,' she decided happily, dwelling on the wee collection, 'I'll think of something.'

It Takes All Sorts

Letters home often convey greater warmth on tape than those that have been penned, particularly if the handwriting of the sender is not exactly copperplate. Two examples taped by Ulster expatriates help to prove the point. This one was from Baltimore:

'Hello there, Maggie, and all the others in Ballymacarrett. This is me. As I tole you in my last tape, Baltimore is the rare place. Them motor cars wud take you to the fair so they would. They all luck like hearses and whizz all over the place, waitin' like wild animals to run ye down, and then go aff like mad to get somebody else. Ye wudden credit it. Ye'd think they were all driv by undertakers.

'Yer morr's still findin' it hard to get used to everything. She still misses boiled spuds in their jackets an', wud ye believe it, sits there in front of the bax longin' for a quarter of liquorice allsorts. The orr day she said she'd love a cuppa tea and a sore head. As for caffy for her breakfast, she says it's like what savages would drink.

'It's a scream when we take her out. We went intil a shap for a pair of shoes for her an' she tole the girl she didden want the soles to be made of paper.

'The poor girl had to lissen to her tellin' about her fren from Conlig who nivver wore his boots till he walked in them for a day or two. She had the whole shap in stitches

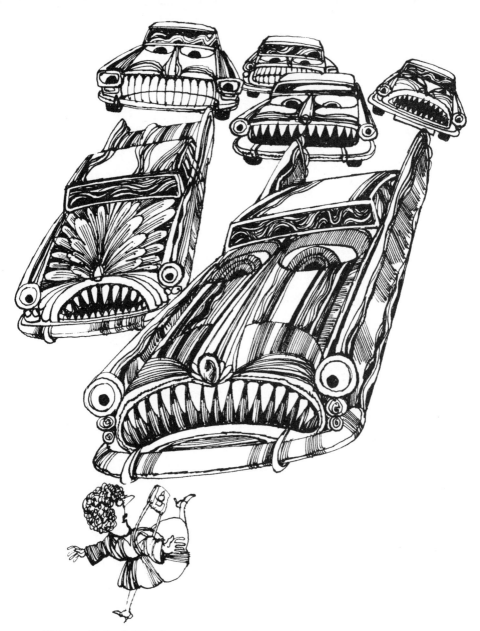

*'They all luck like hearses and whizz all over the place, waitin'
like wild animals to run ye down.'*

when she said, "I want a pair that when I set fut in a place I'll luck as if I'm enjoyin' myself and not sufferin' agony."

'The way she keeps on cummin' out with the oul sayins is a riot. How she minds them all is beyond me, but there's no stappin' her. She got talkin' to a policeman one day when she was out for a walk. It started to rain an' she says to him, "A wise man haps himself up if it's teemin'." We thought he was goin' to lift her.

'She tole our windy cleaner, "Any woman who tells you she'll be on her in a minnit won't be half-an-hour early." We went to do a bitta shappin' and when I was buyin' some bananas she comes out with, "It's a dear honey that's licked aff the whins."

'Still she's great crack. Home and the green grass of Dundonald Cemetery is nivver far away when she's aroun'.'

Another tape, this time from Oregon, ran:

'An' how's are Eleanor? How are yiz all gettin' on? You would take your enn at some of the people here. The girl next door came in till see us the orr night and I can tell you she was a right one. Looked like somebudy outa "Dallas". Her white teeth and her lipstick were stickin' out.

'She was wearin' green eye shadda that was the colour of Dan McGuigan's medda. I'm not tellin' ye a word of a lie. I said to myself, I said, "There's one waitin' to be swep aff her feet by a man she can daminate."

'She sat there talkin' to us about her legs. That's what they're like here. At home you wudden ever mention yer legs in public. Every other word she came out with was "I guess." It was "I guess this" and "I guess that" the whole time she was in the house. If there had been a guess meter in the house she'd have run up a quare bill, I thought to myself.

'The people here are all right, I suppose. They're always in a rush. They just don't know what a wee dander means.

But then I suppose it takes all sorts, doesn't it? All the best
from Oregon.'

A Right Pair

A lamplighter and a flute player would not appear to have a great deal in common, seeing the former had a tin ear and the latter earned his living as a window cleaner. Yet they deserve to be linked, if only for their Ulster identity.

The flute player was encountered in the crowd waiting for the return of the marchers in a Twelfth of July procession. This is how the incident was described to me:

'There was this wee man who started talking to me. He told me he was eighty-seven and came from Armagh, where my mother was born. When he mentioned having been a bandsman I asked him if he remembered a tune called "The Moon Behind the Hill".

' "Indeed I do," he said. "Man I do that. Them were the days when I was in the flute band. I never missed a march or a rehearsal. The flutes cost us only two shillings apiece. They were great wee instruments but I saved up five shillings, half a week's wages, and bought one that had a couple of extra keys. I had been told about the value you could get out of them.

' "I was the only man in the band to have one like it. I thought it was great. When the band was booked to play anywhere I used to fill it up with olive oil the night before and cork it up. The next day it would have the loveliest mellow tone you ever heard. Many a time I've thought of writing to James Galway to tell him but I didn't like."

'I used to fill it up with olive oil.'

'At that minute the lambegs arrived and I told him they could do with him and his flute. His eyes twinkled. "You're right there so you are," he said. "But I've got out of the way of it now. Know what I'm going to tell you? I have six sons. Every one of them has a car but not a single one of them plays the flute. Isn't it funny?" I could hardly hear him for the lambegs.'

The lamplighter, Geordie McGlinchey, operated in East Belfast. Everybody knew Geordie. He had a blind younger brother who always accompanied him on his rounds. 'The exercise is good for Shooey,' Geordie said.

Shooey made baskets for the Workshops for the Blind and was a regular patron of the branch public library for a book in Braille. He had been born blind. 'A great pity of him,' people said, 'for he's a fine figure of a man.'

Geordie they knew as a 'dacent man'. He kept pigeons and had been a widower for many years. His wife died of cancer. She played the piano at Sunday School concerts. Geordie often said, 'We're a right pair. Here's me with a tin ear and there was her, fantastic on a piano.'

Geordie often wished he could own a pub. 'If it ever comes about,' he said, 'I'd call it *The Latherin*. When I was a wee lad my mother used to tell me when we were having our tea, "Latherin there, Geordie." It would mind me of her.'

'A funny world,' he once said. 'Here's me bringin' light to the dark streets and yet I can do nathin' for my poor brother, livin' out his days in the dark. God moves in mysterious ways. There's nights I could go roun' smashin' all the windys in sight with that pole of mine just to show what I think of the bad luck a man can have.

'Then I say to myself, things cud be worse. I could be blind and Shooey could be the lamplighter. And then he cud have joined the Army and been aff to see the world. And where would I be then?'

An

Inasent Party

Statements on tape held in Magherafelt RUC Barracks concerning an accident involving two petrol driven vehicles on 10 February:

I, Constable Archibald Gordon, hereby state:

Arthur Morrison was driving a Fiat in the direction of Magherafelt when he and the Cortina driven by William Mehaffey were in collision. It was raining at the time but it was nothing more than a slight skiff. When Mr Mehaffey was giving his version of the accident he sounded as if he had drink taken but a breathalyser test proved negative. He denied that he failed to drive with due care. Mr Morrison says that the fault lay with Mr Mehaffey who, he alleged, had not been looking where he was going. Both cars suffered slight damage but neither driver sustained injury. I came to the conclusion that Mr Mehaffey was the driver at fault.

Taped statement by Arthur Morrison, retired bank official:

I was driving my Fiat at approximately 40 miles an hour, well on my own side of the road. There was a straight stretch ahead and it was raining slightly. There was no other traffic in sight until suddenly I saw this vehicle approach. It was not on its proper side of the road and to my surprise the driver appeared to be looking at cattle grazing in a field alongside. He was travelling at around 50 miles an hour and I sounded my horn to warn him but he kept on at the same speed, heading straight for me.

I saw that a collision was inevitable so I applied my brakes and swerved. Unfortunately he kept on the same course and our vehicles scraped past each other before my car went into the hedge. I did everything humanly possible to avoid the man but it was of no avail. When I saw him getting out of his car with an orange kitten perched on his shoulder I could hardly believe my eyes. I had great difficulty in keeping myself from castigating him in no uncertain terms. It is obvious he should not have been allowed on the Queen's highway, not only a danger to himself but a menace to others.

Taped statement by John Mehaffey, cattle dealer:

I am goin' along mindin' my own business when it happened. I'm an inasent party, Constable. As God is my witness it wussen my falt, so it wussen. I onny drive on thee-star so I cudden hev been goin' at a helluva lick at the time. Sure my Ford Vesta's nathan but a bunlascrap. Even on tow it cudden get up speed. I cud see that the orr lad was a four-star boy and I spot him cummin' at me like a bat outa hell in his red Fate. As red as a rooster's comb, so it was. I put on my brakes for I nivver was one to go luckin' for trouble. The next minnit I'm hut. That oul Fate of his swipes me along the side and he's intil the sheugh, harp six as nate as ninepence. I sez to myself, this won't do his rheumatiz any good, if he hes any. Nat a shadda of doubt but the man was outa his mine. Shudden hev been allowed on the road at all.

Me, I was ferly shuck. I had a wee kitten on the sate beside me I was takin' home to the wife. The poor wee animal thlught it was senfor. It let out a shriek and the next minit there it was wrapped roun' my neck, shivverin'.

So that's what happened and the same boyo can argify till the cows come home and it won't make wan bit of difference. He was goin' like the hammers, no matter what he ses. When I tried to give him a haun to get outa his car I ast him what he hed been thinkin' about. The carnaptious bugger didden even thank me. He says, 'Ye shudden be let on the road.' I giv him a look an' tole him right back to his teeth 'Do you mine?' Thank God all I felt when he hut me was a wee dunt on my hinch but it was a quare close shave and me an inasent bystander onny takin' home a wee kitten for the wife, who is a woman awful fond of animals.

The Stewarts

Everybody knew them as The Stewarts. Nobody had a bad word to say about them. They had never married but this was never held against them.

Maggie and Agnes lived on the Fermanagh mountainside on a small farm inherited from their father. He died at the age of ninety-one, one year to the day after burying his wife, after whom Agnes had been named.

Maggie was the elder by three years. There was no nonsense about Maggie, people said, but she was a woman with a heart of corn. Of Agnes they said, 'A girl anybody would warm to.'

Agnes had nearly married when in her late twenties. It had been a period of crisis for the sisters over what would happen when the wedding finally took place. Maggie had made it clear that it was out of the question for the newly-weds to live at the farm, as they proposed. If Agnes married, she and her husband would have to set up house elsewhere.

'It's the wise thing to do,' Maggie argued. 'I've thought it out.'

'But you'd never be able to manage on your own,' Agnes said. 'You'd be awful lonely. All by yourself. Wile lonely on a winter's night.'

Maggie was adamant. 'I'd be all right so I would. You and George would be far far better by your two selves. I'd only be in your road. It wouldn't be fair to George to have two women trippin' him.'

71

'George wouldn't mind one bit. I know George. Anyway, a man is needed about the place. If there wasn't, the time would come when we wouldn't be able to do all the work ourselves. I've often thought about it.'

'Agnes dear, we would have two pairs of hands.'

'We have now.'

'I'm thinkin' as much of George as of you,' persisted Maggie. 'I want the two of you to be happy. George is a fine man. If the two of you were to live here I wouldn't like to have it on my conscience if I was ever to blame for things not workin' out, if it was my fault.'

'George is sure it'll work out. George understands. So do I.'

There were many such discussions before Maggie at last gave way. She did so reluctantly. Although she did not admit it, she yielded because she did not want to have it on her conscience that her stubbornness might be to blame for shattering her sister's romance.

'They don't look like sisters,' people often said of The Stewarts. 'They get on terrible well considerin' they're sisters,' it was also said.

Maggie may have been the elder, with the status that went with it, but it was never made to appear that her seniority meant laying down the law with a heavy hand. It was a happy relationship.

She took three teaspoonfuls of sugar in her tea. Agnes took only one, and liked her tea weak. Maggie's taste was for toast done on both sides. Agnes preferred the one-sided kind. They always slept in the same bed. Agnes was always nearest the window. Maggie filled the two hot water bottles. Agnes always emptied them.

Sex was a subject never talked about. It was carefully avoided ever since Maggie's experience at fourteen with a fertiliser salesman. All that was ever said of it was that 'he took liberties.' 'He scared the wits out of her,' was all Agnes ever heard of it.

The date for the wedding of Agnes and George was duly fixed and arrangements made for the new demands on accommodation in the farmhouse. Maggie secretly retained her doubts about it all. Agnes was in seventh heaven. All would be well, she was sure.

Two weeks before the wedding George and some of his friends had a celebration. 'You're a lucky man,' he was told. 'The luck's hangin' out of ye. You're the boyo. Two women for the price of one! How did you manage it?'

George took it all in good spirit — in more senses than one. There had been a bottle of twelve-year-old. All agreed that it went down well. The party finished late. George set off for home, where he lived with his widowed father and two older brothers. He was in the tractor he used often on the narrow hilly roads. Unluckily, on this occasion it did not seem to respond to the controls as quickly as when he was cold sober. Tractors have a habit of falling on top of the driver when involved in an accident. This one conformed to the pattern. George's body was found in a six-foot ditch four hours after he had left his boisterous friends, the friends who had said he was the lucky man.

If Maggie was unable to resist the feeling that the accident was a blessing in disguise she did not show it. She would never have allowed that. It was unforgiveable to think like that about her sister's heartbreak. For weeks she hated herself for having the thought at all.

Romance never again showed signs of blossoming at The Stewarts. It had been like a warning.

The Stewarts' three cows became six. They were joined by a bull, a donkey, two dogs, and also a horse and trap, which was considered invaluable for journeys into the town and more dependable than a motor car. The bull was named Malcolm because Malcolm McAteer, who sold it to them, had been unexpectedly reasonable about the price. Some said he fancied Maggie, but this was only talk.

Maggie was the expert when it came to the animals. Agnes looked after the hens, milked the cows, gave Malcolm a wide berth, and reigned in the kitchen. Maggie often said she couldn't stand the cooking but would have loved to have been a vet.

Life was hard but bearable for the sisters as the years passed. They were in bed every night before ten o'clock and usually got up and about before seven in the morning. They had a radio but never got around to television, although they had electricity.

They were part and parcel of the quiet, windswept area, always there. People would drop in on them the odd time. They were always made welcome. The sisters weren't talked about because there was little to be said about them. They were two harmless old maids, no bother to anybody. Not like some people.

Sometimes the talk between them would touch on the way the years were creeping up on them.

'If I go before you how on earth will you manage?' Maggie would ask. 'It worries me.'

Agnes would laugh. The memory and the pain of the good-natured George had thankfully dimmed. 'I'll get by. I'll no' be a worry for ye, Maggie dear, for there you'll be in the Lord's bosom as happy as Larry.'

'Don't say things like that. No matter about the bosom of the Lord, I'll worry about ye.'

'Onyway, I'll have no time for the frettin'. I'll have plenty to think about looking after the place. When a body's busy you haven't a minute to sit turnin' things over in your mind.'

It was too much for Maggie. 'Oh Agnes!' she exclaimed, and burst into tears.

'Everything will be all right,' Agnes protested. 'Don't worry your head. Wipe your eyes. If somebody came to the door what would they think?'

74

It was enough to make Maggie get her feelings under control, even if the chances of a knock at the door were as remote as the possibility of a visit from Mrs Thatcher.

Came the worst winter they had known for years. There were four days of snowfalls. Many roads were impassable. The sisters worked tirelessly to see that the livestock had food. For nearly a fortnight it was out of the question to attempt the journey into town.

The weather took its toll of the livestock. Six of the flock of fourteen hens perished. The donkey failed to survive an encounter with a snowdrift. One of the dogs was found dead in its kennel. Then there was the disastrous discovery that Malcolm had fallen into a deep ditch and his frantic threshing to get out had been too much for him. To Maggie his loss was a catastrophe.

'Poor Malcolm,' she lamented. 'Och but wasn't he the great wee animal. I can't bear thinking of the poor thing threshing his wee heart out and nobody near to help him. If only we had known.'

'It would have made no difference,' Agnes said. 'We could never have been able to save him. The weight of him would have been too much for us.'

'All the same.' Maggie was not to be comforted. 'I only wish we had known.'

Even when the minister, on learning of her distress at the loss, called to express his sympathy it seemed to him that she had accepted the blow with less than her usual fortitude. The Reverend Gorman had always regarded Maggie as the less sentimental of the sisters.

Afterwards, talking to his wife about his visit, he said, 'I thought it astonishing. When I was sitting there having a cup of tea with them, Agnes said, "We still have the three cows, Maggie. And the horse and the dog." '

'And what did Maggie say?' his wife asked.

' "I know we have," she agreed. She was looking out of the

window at her grazing cattle. Then she said the most extra-ordinary thing. She said, her eyes on the livestock, "But now Malcolm's gone I wonder which of us will be next?" What could I say to that?'

An Ulster Harascope

*CAPRICORN (Dec 21-Jan 20) Restrain your weakness for opening your big mouth. It makes sense, though, to keep a nopen mine when buckets of cold water are thrown on your ideas. The person you think looks like something that fell out of a crow's nest could turn out to be your fren for life.

*AQUARIUS (Jan 21-Feb 19) Don't be afraid of a challenge. You could be on the pig's back if you meet it. Getting the notion that someone you feel is too forward is out to slit your throat will get you nowhere. If you're gawn on anyone don't be too easily put aff. Play it by ear. You'll find yourself taking your end at where it gets you.

*PISCES (Feb 20-Mar 20) Beware of deciding that your neighbours aren't up to much. Be prepared for an invitation to a wedding or a celebration. It could be better than you think. They could be having the drink outa glass glasses. If there's a chance of a wee bit of stir jump at it. A night's crack is the quare mark.

*ARIES (Mar 21-Apr 20) It is stupid to think that you know a creep when you see one. It isn't always so easy to spot them. If you take pride in a reputation for having a heart of corn don't forget that it can cost you. Your feeling that there aren't many like you in half a dozen could get you into bad odour. Maddesty doesn't do a bit of harm.

*TAURUS (Apr 21-May 21) Don't keep going ram stam at things. It could lead you up the garden. Slow down the music and have a titter of wit. Avoid listening too readily to people who have neither in them nor on them. Slabbering over spilt milk is a waste of time. It is as bad as going over the moon about someone who is no good.

*GEMINI (May 22-June 21) Keep your delight in a fog feed in hand. You'll have it said of you that you have a tape worm you could fly a kite with. It is one of the drawbacks to never being behind the door when there's a good pan on. Avoid jumping to conclusions. The person

you dismiss as having a neb like the cooter of Jimmy McNutt's plough could be dead on.

*CANCER (June 22-July 21) Play it with thowl head when involved in a project costing a lot of money. There are times, however, when you could be passing up a golden opportunity to make a fortune by being over cautious. You are probably a person of whom your ma once said you were a stern wee thing. It behoves you to realise that violins can light you in the soup.

*LEO (July 22-Aug 22) When you are beside yourself it is useful to realise that there's a latta sallus in a garden. Remember thowl sayin' that brass pounds don't just grow on trees. Learn to be more punctual. In the morning don't shout 'Mup' when you're still in bed.

*VIRGO (Aug 23-Sep 23) You may have been a wheeker at hankie football but that isn't going to send your bank manager into hysterics of admiration about your overdraft. Only a bampot imagines that a steady job can fall into one's lap. If you sit thinking long all the time you could be in it up to your oxters.

*LIBRA (Sep 24-Oct 23) It doesn't make sense to go through life looking as if you'd spent the night in an abattoir just because you've been stood up. Wise people shove their disappointments in the attic. It creates a poor impression to make people feel that shaking hands with you is like shaking hands with a sockful of porridge.

*SCORPIO (Oct 24-Nov 21) Use your loaf about imagining that the colleague you admire will always have time for you. Just because you get a buzz from someone it doesn't follow that they won't look on you as a glype of the first water. Don't lose the bap if you find out. Make a note: Oul lip will get you nowhere.

*SAGITTARIUS (Nov 22-Dec 21) Beware of the danger of being too pass-remarkable. To say of a neighbour, 'That man has ears on him like Doherty's donkey' could lead to your having the other side of your face lifted. Be especially careful about the way you behave at a drinks party. Keeping a civil tongue in your head has helped to pay the mortgage before this.